ARNE & CARLOS

Make Your Own
Ideabook

Create Handmade Art Journals and Bound Keepsakes to Store Inspiration and Memories

Photography: Ragnar Hartvig

TRAFALGAR SQUARE
North Pomfret, Vermont

First published in the United States of America
in 2016 by
Trafalgar Square Books
North Pomfret, Vermont 05053

Originally published in Norwegian as *Boka du lager selv*

Copyright © 2015 Cappelen Damm AS
English translation © 2016 Trafalgar Square Books

The instructions and material lists in this book were carefully reviewed by the authors and editor; however, accuracy cannot be guaranteed. The authors and publisher cannot be held liable for errors.

ISBN: 978-1-57076-761-6

Library of Congress Control Number: 2015960382

Illustrations and collages: Arne & Carlos
Photography: Ragnar Hartvig
Stylist: Ingrid Skaansar
Book Design: Lisa Mosveen
Translation: Carol Huebscher Rhoades

Printed in China
10 9 8 7 6 5 4 3 2 1

CONTENTS

5
Foreword

PREFACE

It's all about the joy of owning one book or several, and how nice it is to leaf through all types of paper, sewn together by you and for you. This book shows you how to make and use your own homemade ideabooks.

We've heard about the "paperless society," but we think paper is no less important now than it ever was. There are beautiful books and magazines that are all about the paper. Paper continues to make people happy. Reading with a tablet or computer can't compare to the feeling of owning and holding a book. Every home should have some bookshelves—and some books to put on them.

You can collect your thoughts, recipes for cooking, inspiration for handcrafts, notes, secrets, and pictures in your own hand-made ideabooks. You can glue in tickets and cuttings from tours you've been on, holidays you've taken, places you've visited. Make your own notebooks nice and thick with soft and ragged edges, and fill them with ideas and memories. Glue and repair spines and cracks between the pages, because you'll want to put in everything—and that can be a little hard on a book. And what do we mean by "ideabook"? A book you've made yourself can hold anything you want! It could, for example, be a memory book, a planning book, a renovations book, or perhaps a gardening book.

Well-worn books are like old people—they are lovelier because they've lived a life with good memories!

Most people who work creatively have one or more such books. Some are satisfied with a loose-leaf system. They place page after page in a ring binder or preserve the papers in folders; others collect their papers in plastic document folders or glue their chosen memories in sketch books. We've sewn and created our own ideabooks for many years, and used these books to document all aspects of our creative lives.

To look into our ideabooks is the nearest one can come to looking into the creative right sides of our brains. We welcome you in!

ARNE&CARLOS

(PART 1)

Chapter 1

INTRODUCTION

We've always been interested in the process that leads to the design of a product, more than in the finished product itself. We like to find concepts, dig up history, and seek out illustrations for inspiration, all of which we assemble in collages and resource pictures.

Originally we worked most with resource pictures that we hung on the wall. However, in 2002, when we were working on the design of a clothing collection inspired by origami, we had so many thoughts and ideas that we couldn't limit ourselves to just a few collages. We got a photo album and began filling the pages with collages and other things related to paper folding. We added text to our thoughts and supple-

mented our notes with pictures from magazines, fabrics, and our own drawings. The book grew as the collection took shape, and, when we were finished, we also had a journal—an ideabook—that documented the entire design process. It's been years since that project was completed, but we still leaf through that book regularly to find more inspiration. It was also when the concept of our ideabooks was born.

Here are some pictures of the collages/resource pictures that we made up to 2002.

Candy Floss and Cotton Candy. 2001

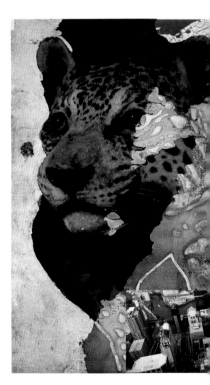

Jungle City, 2000

Toreador, 2001

Women in the Greenhouse, 2002

Back to Nature, 1999

What we especially liked about our first ideabook was how thick it got! It overflowed with collages, pictures, fabric samples, and folded paper, all sticking out between the pages. After a while, the book was so full and had been through so much that it was nicked and had cracked covers and torn edges. The book itself became a symbol of all the creativity and chaos that go into a design process. It was as if what went on in our heads had been transformed into pictures and glued into the book. It gave us a taste for more, and the desire to develop more of our work using ideabooks.

The creative process follows us all through our daily lives—to create is to be "on" all day long. You cannot be

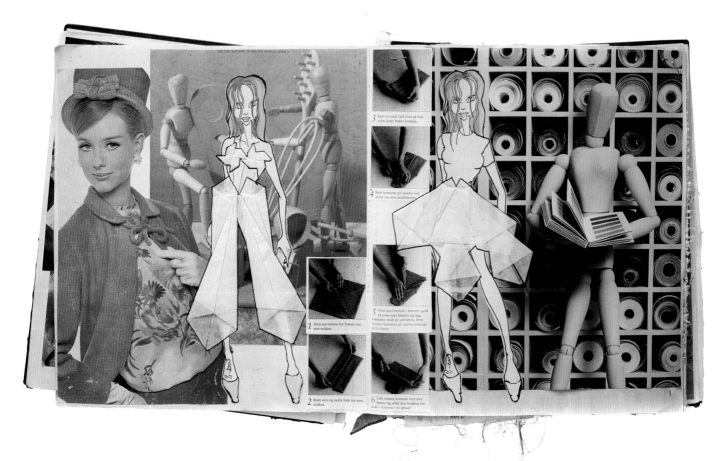

creative if you are only on the job from eight to five. It quickly became evident that the photo albums we'd used for our first ideabooks were altogether too big and heavy, and weren't practical to take everywhere with us. We began thinking about buying some smaller notebooks, but we didn't find anything that we thought would be good enough for such a project. Ideabooks need to be sturdy and tolerate a lot, but at the same time they should be pretty to look at, and have covers that match the contents well.

So we conceived the idea of making and binding the books ourselves, and developed our own homemade technique for doing that.

We used old photo albums for our early ideabooks. These got a little too big to carry around on our travels. This book was made for our clothing collections in 2002 and 2003, and the summer 2004 Origami collection.

One page from the Origami ideabook fell out of the photo album, but that doesn't matter. We like well-used and worn books.

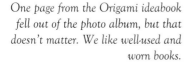

RECYCLING

Our first ideabooks were big old photo albums. Eventually we decided to make our own out of recycled paper.

In our attic, we had collected unfinished drawings by children from the art school where Arne taught in the early 2000s. Arne hadn't had the heart to throw the cast-aside drawings into the recycling bin. There was quite a treasure trove up there: beautiful pages with lots of colorful unfinished drawings. The kids had often painted with watercolors, so many of the pages were already cracked and hard. In the true spirit of recycling, we saw the possibilities for giving these drawings new life! Now they have become pretty pages in quite a few ideabooks.

Sometimes, we bind an ideabook for a specific project, but for the most part we work with three or four or five ideabooks in tandem, adding to them a little here and there, totally without a system—in true creative, hodge-podge, and chaotic Arne-and-Carlos style.

A book that's 5.5 x 8.5 (A5)—half a regular sheet of paper, in other words—is practical for taking on our travels. When the ideabooks become too full, we just have to start a new one. It often happens that we have to take the heavy books out of our carry-on luggage at security, because the security people are very suspicious when they see these unusual books on the screen. If the books are in a bag or suitcase, they are passed through the screening a couple of times, and sometimes the bags get opened up and searched by hand. If we are in a hurry and late, we always take our ideabooks out before going through security and put them in their own bin.

IDEABOOKS

We use our ideabooks as sketchbooks, diaries, and creativity banks. Everything interesting that we find is glued into an ideabook. We write down interesting thoughts and collect inspirational pictures: Polaroid photos from trips as well as tickets, souvenirs, sketches, and fabric samples, yarn ball bands, or small crocheted doilies found in antique shops. Everything we need to remember or keep so we don't forget goes in, too, such as small gifts and cards we receive on trips around the world on our book tours. When our airline flights are boring, we find pages where we've drawn people and "dress" them in knitted garments, or chart new knitting projects on graph paper. Even pretty candy wrappers we find on the street when walking around in a town get a place in an ideabook! They have no planning or order and that's exactly what makes them exciting, inviting books to leaf through. Sometimes looking up things can also be good in itself, despite all the disorder.

Creative Chaos. Ideas for knitting designs amongst various labels, bus tickets, calling cards, and shiny pictures.

Chapter 2

MATERIALS
AND TOOLS

We made the method we use to bind our ideabooks as easy as possible, and you don't need to buy sophisticated and expensive tools. It's not the correct and professional way to bind a book, but it works for us—using simple tools that most people already have at home.

YOU NEED A LOT OF PAPER

We have collected and saved paper over a long period of time. We never know what we'll use it for, but as many people already know, you can always find some way to use up what you've collected. Every now and then we go through our boxes of old paper, cut some up, fold some, and sort it all into bundles.

You can use all types of paper, such as old bank statements, copy paper, gift wrap, envelopes, colorful pages from magazines, posters, children's drawings, advertisements, brown paper, or wax paper. Maybe you took a class many years ago and still have all your old notebooks? You've never been able to toss those notebooks because you thought that one day you would read through them again, but your interest has waned and nothing has come of the plans you made. Take out those notebooks and use them for an ideabook. Perhaps in the future, just as you are looking for a place to glue a pretty picture into your ideabook, a little bit of old wisdom from those classes will pop up.

We have just tidied up our work room and old invoices are being recycled as pages in a new ideabook.

1 Bundles of paper tied with a bow and ready to go. The next time we need a new ideabook, we just have to grab a pack of paper and get the sewing machine out. Leafing through such books after they are bound is always exciting, meeting old memories and forgotten notes that pop up.

2 Teaching materials from a class when Arne studied fashion design have also become pages in an ideabook.

3 Adding in some paper smaller than letter size (8.5 x 11/A4); everything can be used. Here we give a bit of brown paper and an envelope new life. Envelopes are good to have in books so you can easily collect tickets, business cards, and anything else you don't want to glue in. Use envelopes to collect items until you get home, because you don't want to take glue along on a trip. Insert an envelope here and there so you'll have practical pockets to hold things that can't be glued in right away—or at all.

4 We never use old paper patterns when we make clothing, but we collect the old pages of printed patterns. Interesting pictures become glued in and the pattern sheets end up as pages in our ideabooks. These are decorative and make nice covers. Old pattern sheets from Burda Magazine have become the pages in a new ideabook.

5 Pretty wrapping paper torn into suitable sizes makes several pages in another.

6 Set in the wrapping paper together with white pages to have many fine decorative pages.

PAPERBOARD FOR BOOK BINDINGS

You can use paperboard from drawing blocks or buy readymade paperboard suitable for 5.5 x 8.5 (A5) books at craft stores. The binding should weigh around 22½ oz / 640 grams. Cover the board with fabric or paper.

Your imagination is the limit here! We've made covers out of everything we could think of: Japanese wrapping paper, the burlap bags that you get when you buy rice at the shop, old patchwork fabric that we sewed together, gift paper, old fabric samples, and even fabric remnants that we bought especially for a book—for example, some of our Christmas books are covered with Christmas-themed fabric. It is especially pleasing when the cover gives a little taste of what's inside the book, so why not embroider part of the cover for an ideabook about embroidery? If you think all that glue will be too messy, there are self-adhesive fabrics you can use instead.

Here are some of our ideabooks. These are full of photos, clippings, inspiration, memories, and secrets.

16 BOOK COVERS

On the next 6 pages, we show 16 different ideabook covers that we made based on the unique materials we have collected.

1. *Cotton fabric with Border Collie patterns, found in the patchwork section of a hobby shop somewhere in Denmark.*

2. *A dress fabric from Grandmother's attic.*

3. *An old burlap rice bag has made a fine ideabook cover.*

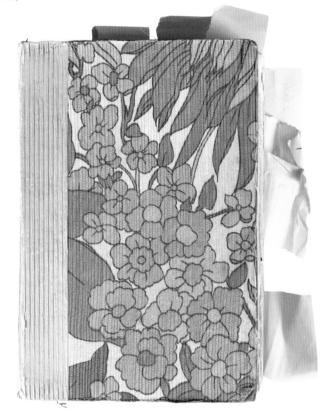

4. *Dress fabric from the 1970s has been given a new life.*

5. *Curtain fabric found in the remainders basket of an interior design business.*

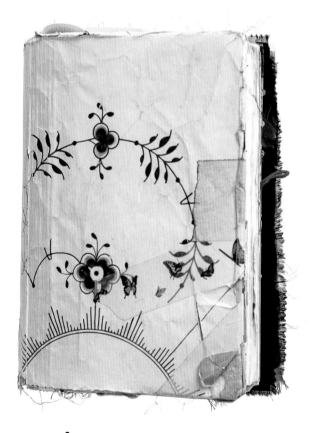

6. *Wrapping paper with straw patterns used as book paper.*

7. *A fabric sample, with sequin embroidery, from
the time when we worked sewing clothing.*

8. *Crazy quilt technique fabric with decorative stitching gives even the smallest piece of fabric some new life for a cover.*

9. *Candy paper from Japan.*

10. *Great-Grandmother's old kitchen curtains.*

11. *Remnant of Chinese fabric from a blouse collection we made in 2004, and wrapping paper ribbon from when we had an internet shop.*

12. *Christmas fabric found in a hobby shop in Seattle.*

13. *Embroidery from heavy leftover yarn glued to a cover.*

14. *Another piece of curtain material from the remnants basket.*

15. *This French fabric was just right for a cooking ideabook.*

16. *Fabric from an old trouser costume from the 1970s. The material was a little too thick to fold around the paper, but too fine not to be used. In this case, the fabric was trimmed edge to edge with the paperboard and wrapping paper from a shop in Florence was torn into strips, glued to the fabric, and folded around the cover as an edging. You can also edge such covers with textile tape.*

THREAD

We use the thread we have on hand when we bind our ideabooks.

When we stitch sections of paper, we often sew many at the same time so we have them on hand when we need them for a new ideabook. If you use different colors of thread, it is simpler to see which thread should be used for the next bundle; but if you are sewing all the sections for a book at the same time, you certainly don't want to change thread for every single bundle you are sewing together. Use up leftovers and empty your sewing box. If you have to buy thread, you might be able to buy small packets containing an assortment of colors at a fabric store. We stitch our sections from the outside—that is, the side of the section that shows when it is folded and where it is sewn together at the end. If we have many white sheets, as for the bottom section of the four in the bundle, we use white bobbin thread and different colors of top thread on the spine so the strands will be easier to find when sewing the spine.

You can also use quilting thread if you want a thicker thread. It's a good idea to sew the spine on by hand with a stronger thread than the one used to stitch the sections together.

SCISSORS, PRECISION KNIFE, RULER, AND CUTTING BOARD

1   We fold and trim the sheets that are too big so they'll fit the book we want to make.

2   Ragged edges are okay.

To get the right size on a sheet of pretty gift paper or something similar, there are many different paper cutters you can cut paper with if you want straight lines. If you want ragged edges on the paper, there are also special cutters you can draw the edges of the paper through so it will look ragged. We fold an approximately straight edge where we will tear the paper in letter-size (A4) sheets, which we fold so it will fit in our book. This also gives "ragged" edges, and since

3   A pretty page from a magazine gets new life. The excess paper is torn off and the paper is folded down the center to make new pages. When folded and placed together with another section, the pictures acquire a completely new look that will be exciting to have in your ideabook.

4   If a page sticks out a little too much, it's okay to trim the paper.

5   For regular paper, hold your fingers on the foldline. If you are using slightly thicker sheets of paper, such as copy paper, a folding tool can help make a sharp fold down the sheets. Some paper can be more difficult to tear well—this bag, for example. Uneven edges on the sheets of paper are also fine.

our books get heavy use and often come with us on trips, they will soon be ragged in any case. Another technique for ragged edges that Carlos learned about when he was little is to place a ruler on a sheet of paper and tear along the side of the ruler. That way you'll get an edge that's straight overall, but still a little bit rough.

GAUZE
BINDING

We use gauze binding that is about 3 in / 8 cm wide, cut to the length needed for the book. Craft stores sell rolls of gauze that will stick well to the spine of the book when you rub glue in. Pharmacies carry a product called elastic gauze bandage that is somewhat more tightly woven and functions well. You can usually buy a packet containing two rolls about 3 in x 4 ⅓ yd / 8 cm by 4 m, which is enough for at least 35 ideabooks of the size we like.

CORRUGATED PAPER

Check your local craft store for corrugated paper in a variety of colors so that you can match your covers. You can also buy large rolls of corrugated paper at office supply stores, which will be plenty for many ideabooks—several hundred, in fact, so that might be a bit too much corrugated paper unless you expect to make a lot of books! It usually comes in unbleached brown and is a little thicker. It's the same type that you often get to protect items for shipping. In the spirit of good recycling, you can also get corrugated paper that has been used as packaging and then recycle it in your books.

GLUE AND
MOUNTING SPRAY

Allround Glue, Quickglue or wood glue—these are strong glues that hold well and are quite suitable for these projects.

If you want to decorate the pages with stencils, you'll need mounting spray. Without such a spray, the painting under the stencil and the pattern can bleed out. You can find mounting spray in art or office supply stores.

Whenever we glue in pictures that will cover the whole page or go over two pages, we also use mounting spray. Larger pictures glued in with regular glue sticks will often end up with air bubbles under the pictures. If, for example, you find a flower picture with many stalks and flowers and you want to cut away the background and only have the

flowers in the book, you need to use mounting spray. If you try to use a glue stick for intricate cut-outs, the paper will quickly tear into pieces.

You can also use decoupage glue such as Royal Coat's finish. It's fun to glue in things with decoupage glue. Everything you glue in will look very nice and the surface will be sealed. When you use this glue on a thin sheet of paper, it will make the paper rough and stiff, so if you are working with thin paper, try gluing several sheets together to have thicker pages in the book. We have some pages in our ideabooks that are glued with Royal Coat Decoupage Finish and we think the bumpy paper is very charming.

The size of the needle on the sewing machine isn't very important as long as you can pass the thread through the eye. We normally use needles that are Size 80. It's not necessary to use a sharp new needle when you are sewing paper; old needles may actually work better, but you should make sure the thread fits first.

SEWING MACHINE

We decided to use an old crank Singer sewing machine in the pictures for this book because it's so photogenic. We also have pedal-driven machines. Our favorite is the old Husqvarna sewing machine from Arne's grandmother, purchased in the 1970s. It is a solid machine that holds its own really well. You don't need more than that.

You need a simple sewing machine that can sew straight seams with long stitches. If you don't already have a sewing machine, it's absolutely not necessary to go out and buy one of the expensive, high-tech machines, unless you plan to use it for other more advanced sewing projects later. You can find a simple machine at a good price in a second-hand shop. The old, heavy sewing machines were often very high quality, so you shouldn't have to look too far to find a machine that is quite good. Since sewing has become more and more popular, you can also find inexpensive, newly-produced sewing machines these days. IKEA sells a model for around $70, but we've also seen functioning old crank machines for the same price in antique shops.

If you can't sew and have never used a sewing machine, this project gives you a good chance to try it, since you don't need any specialized knowledge about sewing. You only have to sew straight seams with long stitches. All you need to learn is how to thread the machine and adjust the stitch length.

If you don't want to machine stitch the sections, you can sew them by hand. In that case, fold the paper in the center, draw a line, punch holes with an awl and sew into the holes.

PRESSES

A few years ago we were at a second-hand shop and found a lovely little (but also heavy) iron press. We were not totally sure if it was a book or a flower press but it has done a good job of pressing our books. If you don't have access to a similar press and it will be difficult to find one, you might be able to buy a simple press (consisting of two plates with screws in the corners) at a craft store. If you can't find one of those either, there is no need to worry. All you have to do is make your own press: Place the book between two wooden boards, and secure the boards tightly around the book with two clamps.

Here are our three variations of a book press. At the left is the fine, heavy iron book press that we bought at an antique store. In the center is a home-made variation made with two clamps and two boards. To the right, an old wooden press.

Chapter 3

HOW TO SEW
YOUR BOOK

We work with letter-size (A4) sheets that are folded in half (A5) in this book. If you want a different size, just work on the same principles but adjust for your paper size.

A LITTLE ABOUT SIZES

Four sheets are folded into a section and then folded once more in the opposite direction to make a good line to sew through. Make 15 sections.

If you want an even larger book, you can fold larger sheets down to tabloid (11 x 17/A3) or letter (8.5 x 11/A4) size. The covers should always be ⅜ in / 1 cm longer and ¼ in / 0.5 cm wider than the sections.

Our books are always made with 15 sections and each section consists of four letter-size (A4) sheets folded at the center to 5.5 x 8.5 (A5) size. That makes 16 pages in each section. If you want larger sheets in the book (for example, pretty gift wrap), cut or tear off the excess so you have one or more letter-size (A4) sheets that are then folded edge to edge to 5.5 x 8.5 (A5) size.

SEWING THE SHEETS OF PAPER

When you have folded your sheets of paper into sections, you are ready to sew them together down the center. We sew four and four sheets of paper because it makes a suitable thickness for the sheets when they are folded and is a good thickness for sewing. You can use any sewing thread you have, unless it's very old; check to make sure it hasn't darkened.

You'll need a sewing machine if you don't want to sew by hand. All of our ideabooks are stitched by machine. You can use a brand new machine or an old crank one. Our old crank handle machine is nice for this—it is pretty to look at and it doesn't break. It only makes straight seams and that's all you need. Check to make sure you've set the machine to the longest stitch length. Tight stitches can tear the paper. Make sure that the needle and bobbin are threaded correctly and adjust if necessary. It's a good idea to use a color of bobbin thread that will look nice against the color of the paper. White thread on white paper can be difficult to find again on the folded edge when you sew the book on the spine. If the seam is somewhat uneven, just make an extra fold on the paper and force the seam to lie on top of the fold. You can use a folding tool if the paper is a little thick.

Leave long end threads when you begin to sew and also make sure you leave long tail ends when you finish the seam.

When you have sewn the sheets of paper together and have enough sections for the thickness you want for your ideabook, it's time to tie the sections together.

KNOTTING THE
END THREADS

1   Place the sections of paper together and tap the spine against the table a few times so all the bundles are
    aligned with each other.

2   Use grip clamps or hold the book between your knees and knot the section threads at one end of the spine
    together. Tie the threads from the first section to the threads from the second section, the threads from the
    second section to those of the third, and so on, until all the sections have been tied together. Tie everything
    once more to be sure it's all secure.

3   Tie the threads on the other end the same way.

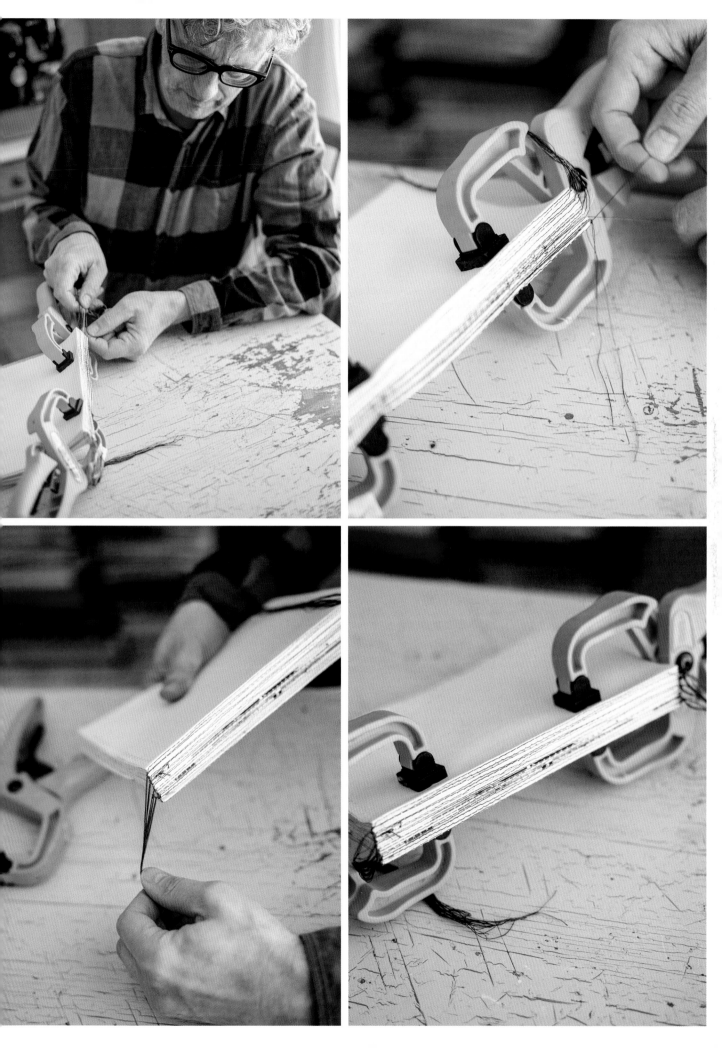

BINDING THE SECTIONS OF PAPER TOGETHER

You'll need a needle that's thin but not too long for sewing on the spine. Use heavy-duty thread such as Coats & Clark X-tra Strong Upholstery Thread for this job to make the backing stronger.

If you are having difficulty holding the sheets of paper together while you sew, you can use universal clamps to make the work easier. Sew under the threads in the spine, tie a knot around the first stitch in the first section and make sure that all the sheets of paper are included in the stitching. Press the paper together extra firmly when the last section of paper is sewn, and tie a knot around this stitch before you sew back through the sections, approx. ⅝ in / 1.5 cm from the first seam. Continue to sew the same way back and forth until the entire spine is sewn. Finish with a knot around the last stitch in the outermost section. If you are holding the sections of paper between your knees, you will need to tap the spine against a table to even out the spaces that can quickly form between the sections.

A completely sewn spine, ready for gluing.

Use Allround glue, Quickglue, or wood glue. Coat the spine thoroughly.

GLUING THE SPINE

1   Use your finger to rub the glue in well along the spine of the book.

2   Bring the end threads up/down onto the spine and rub them into the glue.

3   Add some extra glue if the spine feels dry.

4   You'll need some gauze binding for the spine, or you can use anything you have that is similar to the gauze. Add some extra glue and rub it in all over.

5   Trim the gauze to the correct length and rub it into the spine.

6   Make sure the gauze is centered on the spine.

7   After the spine has been glued, leave the book to dry.

8   Once we get going, we like to sew several ideabooks at a time. It's always great to have some half-finished ideabooks ready whenever we need a new one. These books have strips of thin, loosely woven fabric similar to gauze binding. We found this material in a sewing shop many years ago. The fabric was difficult to cut straight so the edges became a little sloppy, but that doesn't matter. The fabric disappears behind the covers when they have been glued on. Gauze on a roll is easier to use. Make sure you have a wide enough piece of gauze for the spine of your book. It needs to be wide enough to slightly overlap the first and last sections. The gauze is the same type you would use for mask making, but without the plaster of Paris—make sure you buy gauze that doesn't have plaster of Paris, because that will not produce good results.

9   You can also decorate the spine of your ideabook by gluing on a little strip of lace or a decorative ribbon at the top and bottom of the spine. That way you'll have a little embellishment that sticks out when the book is completely glued.

COVERS

1   You'll need two pieces of paperboard for the covers. The weight of paperboard we most often use is 22½ oz / 640 g. However, if you cover the ideabook with a thick fabric, you will want to use thinner board. Check the measurements of the book and cut the board so that it is ⅜ in / 1 cm longer than the length of the book and ¼ in / 0.5 cm wider than the width of the book.

2   When gluing the covers on, they should stick out ¼ in / 0.5 cm from the first and last section at the top and bottom edges of the book and ¼ in / 0.5 cm at the front edge of the book. At the spine, the cover should lie edge to edge. We make all our books approximately 5.5 x 8.5 size and our paperboard measures 6 x 8¾ in / 15 x 22.5 cm. You may also find ready-made covers in this size at craft shops.

3   When the covers have been cut, you can "dress" them with fabric or paper. We use fabric remnants of all types or smooth paper that is somewhat heavy. Cut or tear the paper or fabric so that it is approx. 2–2½ in / 5–6 cm larger than the cover. This way you'll have selvedges to fold in when you glue.

4 Cover the entire surface with glue and rub it in well.

5 This is the messiest part, and you can't be afraid to get glue on your fingers! If you don't want to get this messy, use self-adhesive fabric instead.

6 Place the cover centered on the fabric or paper and squeeze some glue into each corner, and then all over. Rub the glue in all over, on both the paperboard and fabric or paper.

7   Fold the corners in over the paperboard.

8   Glue in the sides after you have securely glued in the already-folded corners.

9   Squeeze glue onto the long and short sides, rub it in well, and fold the sides in over the paperboard.

10   Rub and smooth the paper or fabric so that it adheres well to the paperboard.

10

11 Place the prepared and glued covers in a plastic folder and lay them on the press (see photo)—either one on top of the other or side by side, depending on what type of press you have.

12 Screw down the press with all your might.

13 If you have used fabric, you can also cut it so you can lay both covers side by side and use the same piece of fabric for the covers and spine.

14 Glue the corners and the long sides all over, underneath and in the front. Between the covers, place clips to hold the fabric in place while it dries. Leave a space about $^3/_8$ in / 1 cm wider than the thickness of the spine of the book you have sewn and glued. Place plastic folders around the covers and put them in the press. (Without the plastic folders, the covers will be glued together or be glued to the woodwork of your press, or to your two boards.)

15   This pretty press was a find in a second-hand shop. The covers also need to be enclosed in plastic while they dry in a press like this because, without the plastic, the covers can get speckled. Be careful when using colored plastic, because the color might transfer to the book covers. Transparent plastic folders are really good to use for this, and you can easily scrape off any residue if the glue leaks through the fabric or paper.

16   If you have an old wooden press or the like, you can also use that. A cover with the same fabric on both paperboards and the spine can lay flat on a large enough press. Let the covers dry until the next day.

17   Now we've made the covers for two books and can take the evening off. The covers must dry until the next day. If you used self-adhesive fabric for the covers, you don't need to leave it in the press to dry. You can put the covers on the book right away.

17

GLUING THE COVERS ONTO THE BOOK

1 When the covers have dried, remove the plastic and spread the glue well over the first and last pages of the book.

2 Also smooth the gauze from the spine over the sides. Trim any gauze that sticks out at top and bottom.

3 Place the covers precisely on the front and back of the book. They should be edge to edge against the book's spine and ¼ in / 0.5 cm extra should then stick out at the front, top, and bottom of the book.

4 Check to be sure that the book is straight when you glue on the covers. It is so irritating if the pictures in the book are upside down in relation to the motifs on the cover.

5 Trim the corrugated paper or fabric to cover the spine. We usually use corrugated paper.

6 Trim edge to edge with the book at top and bottom. We leave between 1¼–2 in / 3–5 cm in on the covers on both sides. Check to be sure that the corrugated paper folds nicely around the spine.

7 Don't glue too tightly to the spine.

8   When the covers have been glued onto the book, stick the covers into the plastic sheets and close the book, place the whole thing in the press, and let everything dry overnight. Make sure the book is aligned in the press. If it is crooked, the book will not be as nice. The covers must lie straight over each other. Screw the press down well.

9   Books with the same fabric on the covers and spine should be glued the same way. In this case, though, you omit the corrugated paper.

10 Rub the first and last sheets of the book well into the covers.

11 We decorated this book at the top and bottom of the spine, and a little of the decorative ribbon sticks out.

(PART 2)

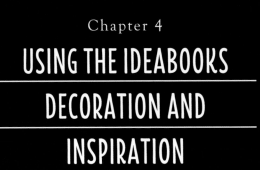

Chapter 4
USING THE IDEABOOKS
DECORATION AND
INSPIRATION

Sweater designs inspired by an old broken flower pot that was decoratively placed in a garden flowerbed.

31 juli 2008

Gensere m.
mønster inspirert
fra den knuste
potta

Hagekanin og
knust potte
sommer
2008

A LITTLE ABOUT
OUR IDEABOOKS

Now you can begin using your ideabooks, and we want to give you somewhere to start. You can decorate the pages just for the sake of embellishment, paint, glue in pieces of paper, print over text, cut out figures, and tint colors. You can find a whole line of art journaling products in hobby shops. We very seldom decorate a page just for the sake of decorating since our books are in constant use.

Our ideabooks are neither organized nor arranged following a theme, because we deal with so many different things at the same time and tend to include a little of everything. We always wish we had been better organized, especially when we have to find something later! Organization would cer-

tainly make it easier to find things again. Sometimes when we've made a new ideabook, the plan is that it should have only one theme, and so the first few pages of the ideabook are very well organized. When ideabooks are not arranged by theme, we often have to leaf through them, but then we

Picture of a sweater with a pretty collar, torn out of a fashion magazine. The drawings we made with hair styles and tattoos inspired by the Inuit were cut out and glued over the sweater picture. An old package of snaps is taped to the page.

might find things we weren't looking for, and that can be useful for new ideas or plans.

We often begin by gluing in pictures or other things we find after cleaning up the writing desk—things we have saved because we like them. You might later end up writing notes over the pictures you glued in at the beginning of the idea-book, but that will give the pictures new life.

Make your own organizer or make one as a present for someone else. Mark off important days and add a picture of a birthday child or other things you want to remember over the course of the year.

Write down notes or make a diary; write in amendments and edits and use different colors. On the days when there isn't much to write about, it can be really nice if you write down the date and the little that has happened, and then frame the text in different colors. Vary the size of the writing and use large and small letters to give life to a page. Perhaps you can find some nice little notebooks with borders, or

another embellishment you like. You could note the days in these and then gradually glue them into an ideabook. You can make fine collages in your ideabook, too.

If you realize that drawing is not your strongest point, you can decorate the pages with various stamps. Clear Stamps has many motifs. Paper tape can be found with many different patterns, and you can use it to decorate with or to attach

pictures to pages. One advantage of this tape is that you can attach things to the book and then remove them later, if you want, without damaging the page. We use a lot of masking tape, which works well to cover up old notes or cover text on recycled paper used as a page. You can write on masking tape and it's fun to use a white-out pen.

The page to the left is from a child's drawing. It was so fine that we left it as is. The colors harmonize well with the butterflies and the washing powder advertisement on the page to the right.

Hair bands work well as bookmarks, and it's always exciting to check pages with hair clips. The more childlike, the better! You can also use large clips for attaching various decorations.

Glue in pretty pictures mixed with embroidered fabric samples and old crocheted doilies. Everything that is in-spiring should get a place in an ideabook. We don't glue in small crocheted doilies; they just lie in loosely. Fabric is glued in or stapled to a page. We have also sewn in fabric remnants with the sheets of paper for a section so the fabric becomes four pages of the ideabook. Everything is possible.

DOODLING

Doodling over a ticket, a postcard, and a souvenir from an exhibit we visited.

Maybe you only doodle with black India ink. Maybe you used to doodle back in the old days, when you sat at the telephone for hours talking nonsense with your friends. It was easy to quickly fill a sheet of paper or a page in the phone book with circles or flowers or abstract curves. Lots of people have certainly doodled during meetings, lectures, or in school. Doodling is just nonsense, arcs and lines. The best doodling comes from idleness and could also be called scribbling. Doodling can make a nice page in an ideabook,

and if you want you can also fill the doodled page with colors. Colorful doodling is really fun—but sometimes it works well and other times it doesn't! If it is especially bad, then all you have to do is glue a picture over it.

Because we are authors, we also use our ideabooks to plan forthcoming books. We plan each page, what type of pictures we want, and how they should be laid out. We keep such pages as is. Some ideas might not be used in the project they were designed for, but can be saved for another time.

16/11-09.

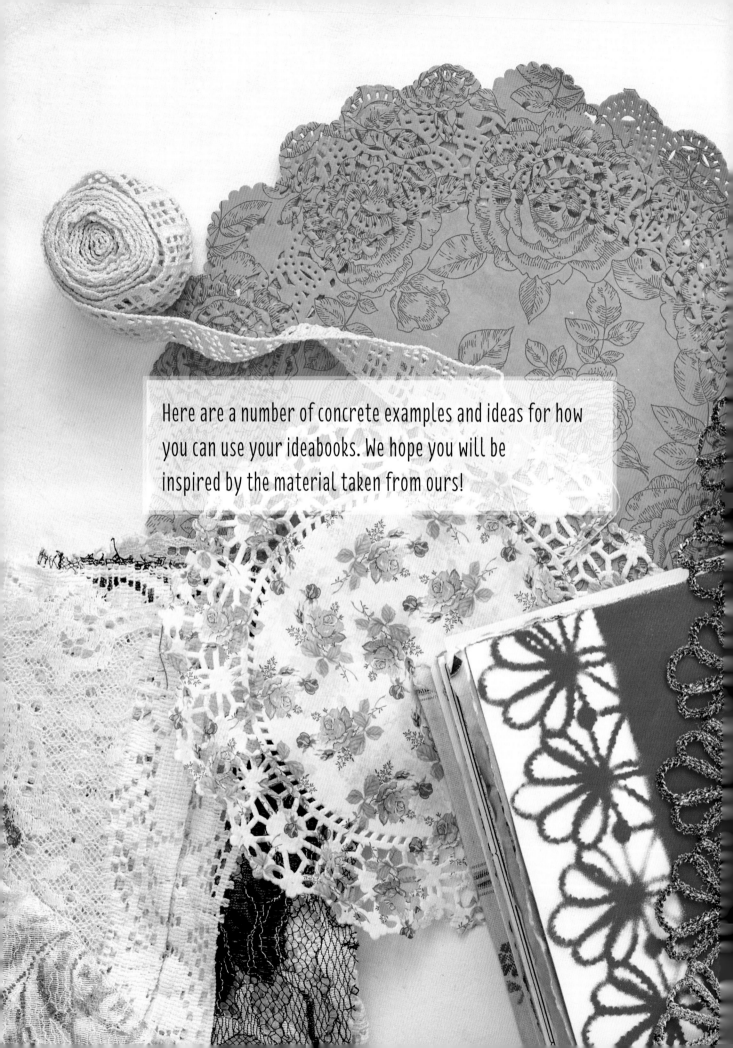

Here are a number of concrete examples and ideas for how you can use your ideabooks. We hope you will be inspired by the material taken from ours!

STENCILS MADE BY LACE AND CROCHETED DOILIES

Make your own stencils with lace, fabric remnants, old ribbons, crocheted doilies, and cake paper doilies.

1 You can lay large pieces of lace fabric over a whole page in a book and spray it all over—or, if you only want to use the lace as an edging, you can easily do that.

2 Cut out a lace strip or use a lace ribbon. Glue the lace along the edge of a letter-size (A4) sheet of paper and let it dry.

3 Lay some paper under the page that will be sprayed and cover the page that won't be painted. Use masking tape between the pages. Spray the lace sheet with mounting spray and position the lace where you want it on the page.

If you want to decorate your pages with stencils, there are many different ones available at hobby shops. Maybe you'd like to use stencils to cover less interesting pages—perhaps a boring advertisement you found in the post that was used for a page in the book. You can easily make your own stencils. We really like our homemade lace stencils and they're exciting to work with. You never know exactly what will result until you spray on the paint and remove the lace. You have to spray textile stencils. We have tried with acrylic paint and a roller, but the fabric is too thick to make good contact with the paper surface. You won't get an impression, just a lot of paint in the lace.

Save old lace, whether from a dress, an old curtain, or a crocheted doily you've never used. Rummage around in

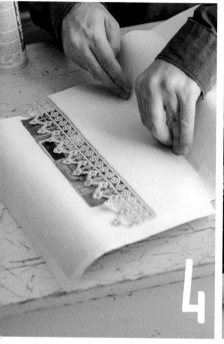  

4 Press the lace down well so the color won't seep under it. Spray over with the color you want.

5 If you are in a hurry, take out the hair dryer and blow on some warm air so the page dries faster.

6 Carefully remove the sheet and see if it reveals some lovely artwork. Remove the paper you used to cover the rest of the book. Be careful when you remove the masking tape so that you don't rip out some of the book.

remainder baskets where they sell fabric, or check out sec-ond-hand stores or shops for recycled goods. Spray the lace with mounting spray, lay it over the page you want to deco-rate, and then spray it with acrylic paint. You can find spray paint at craft stores. You should spray outdoors, when there is no wind. You can spray on a background color first if you want to decorate the whole page. Let it dry and then lay the lace over it. If it has a motif, place the lace so that the motif is where you would like it. Shake the container well before you spray over the page, holding the can approximately 11¾ in / 30 cm away from the page. After you've used the lace a few times and it has become stiff with dry paint, you can cut the pieces to the right size and sew them into an ideabook to serve as pages. These will be pretty pages that just need to be decorated. A little embellishment never does any harm.

Here we glued in a picture we liked and put the lace over it. The lace was sprayed with white acrylic paint. The fun aspect of these stencils is that when you spray them over pictures, the lace will almost look as if it had been cut out with the picture. Snippets of pictures can show through the lace and be very pretty. It can be difficult to stop making pages like this because it's so much fun to see how the lace peeks out from the various backgrounds. Soon there will be many such pages in an ideabook. On the opposite page, we glued in the remnant of a lace ribbon from Paris.

TRANSFERRING
RELIEF RUBBINGS

We had two copying techniques we played with when we were children. One method was to drip wax over pictures in ads and make an impression in the wax; another was to put coins under the paper and rub a pencil over the paper. The old Norwegian five-øre coin had a moose on it—that made for an amusing rubbing!

By using this last technique, you can decorate the pages, preferably before you sew them into the ideabook. Lay your paper over something with a relief design, such as wood blocks with incised patterning or the front covers of old books with engraved designs. You can also make rubbings of textiles and leaves. Use colored pens or a pencil.

When we went on holidays at camping areas, sometimes we made rubbings of wood tables and old logs where people had carved in their names or the date.

We have seen examples of pictures that artists have rubbed. One artist rubbed transfers on the streets in New York and another rubbed brick walls.

If you are using a pencil, you need to secure the sheet so that it doesn't slide around. There is even a fixing spray for this, but if you can't find that, hairspray will work.

KNITTING IDEABOOKS

Of course we begin with knitting and inspiration for knitting designs since that has been our specialty these last few years. When we leaf through our books, we find masses of knitting patterns, old patterns for inspiration, and new patterns we've drawn ourselves.

Patterns from the sock designs we made for Regia. The colors were inspired by Edvard Munch paintings with colors from Norwegian nature.

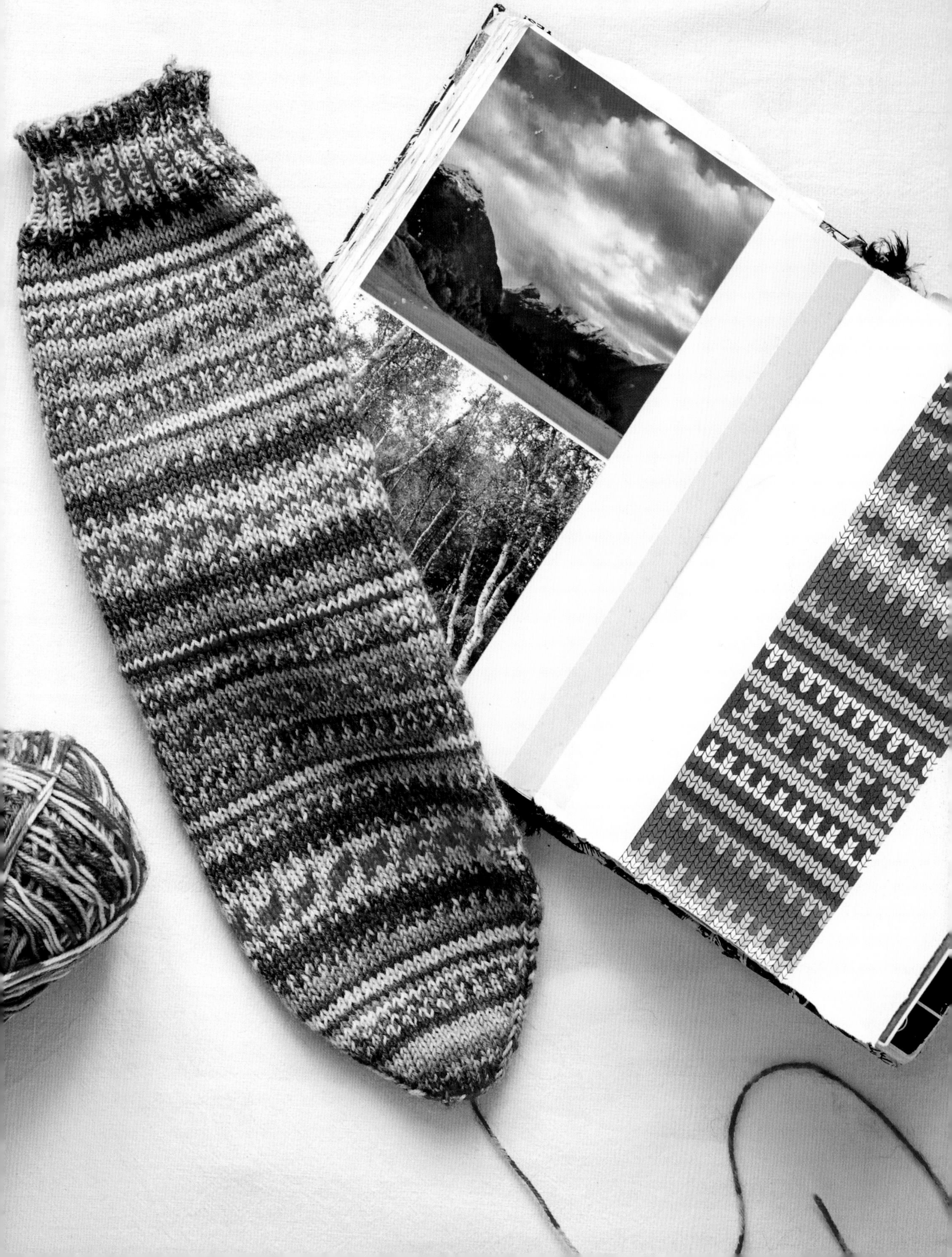

We draw figures without clothes, make several copies of the drawings and then glue them into our books. Then we can draw our ideas onto these whenever they pop up. These are good to have on long trips in case we get bored or discover something new. Many of these sketches don't ever get knitted up, but we keep them all and sometimes we make new designs based on old sketches.

Old knitting inspiration

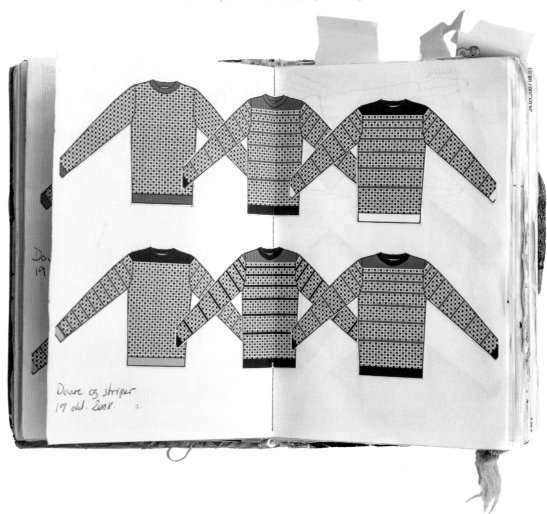

Dawe og striper
19 okt. 2008.   =

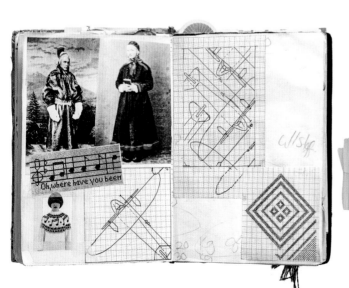

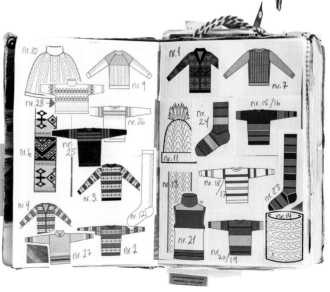

91

CHRISTMAS IDEABOOK

For those of you who celebrate Christmas, make an ideabook and collect everything to do with Christmas—for example, ideas for decorating, recipes, or Christmas-themed handcraft patterns.

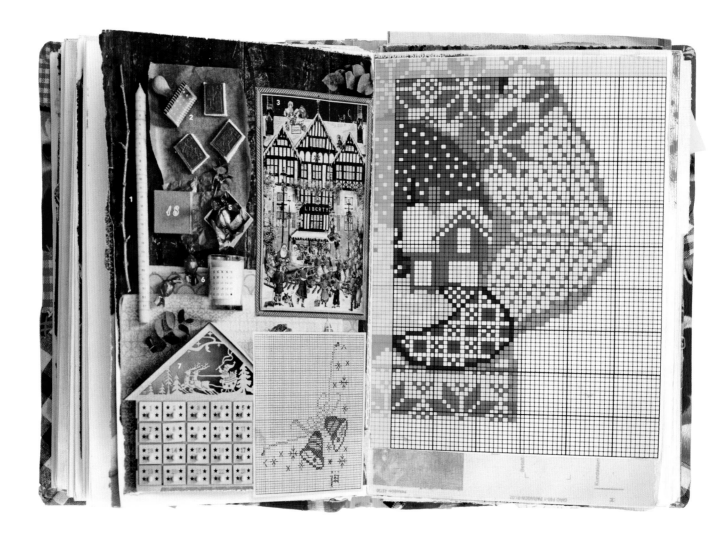

Decorate with glitter and glossy pictures. Keep new and old Christmas cards and glue them in with decorating ideas on sticky notes. Use gift wrap for the pages in your Christmas book. Cut or tear letter-size (A4) sections of wrapping paper and fold it together with copy paper, so you'll have pretty pages with fine patterns spread all through the book.

With doubled Christmas cards, you can lay them in as a sheet of four in a section. If you place the card at the center, you can archive the entire card with both the pictures and greeting—a cozy Christmas holiday puzzle.

CHILDREN'S IDEABOOK

Save your children's drawings and other memories and sew them into a book.

When a proud little artist comes home from daycare or school, the drawings often end up on the kitchen wall or refrigerator door. Some hang there until they turn yellow or fall off. Many are changed out as the years go on. Some small artists might discard a piece before it is finished and want to have some new paper. Save that unfinished artwork, collect it in a shoebox, and take it out when you have enough for an ideabook—or collect the year's productions and put them in a book for that year. Add pictures, baby teeth, and a little lock of hair. Glue in small traces that a child has left behind from the year just past, or earlier years.

Make a pretty memory book with pictures and notes. Use glossy pictures to decorate the pages, glue in stickers, and sprinkle on crystals and glitter.

Perhaps this ideabook will turn into a lovely gift for the child later in life.

These are pages from an old coloring book. They were too nice to cut out or tear so we made copies, decreasing the size so the pages would fit in our ideabook. A childhood memory for inspiration.

COOKING IDEABOOK

Here are the instructions for Arne's favorite
cookies that his grandmother taught him how to bake.
We decided that this recipe would be great for a book
on baking. In this case, you have to make a template
for cutting out the cookies.

If you like to cook, you certainly have recipes everywhere, in cupboards and drawers. Make your own cookbook. Glue in recipes and inspiration. Everyone always has scads of slips of paper with recipes that have been scribbled down quickly during a visit to friends or family. Why not collect all those paper slips into a nice ideabook?

Blemsnipper

1 cup / 240 ml sweet cream
1.1 lb / 17.5 oz/500 g margarine
a pinch of salt
enough flour for the dough

Pour the cream into a large bowl and stir in enough flour for a soft dough. Add the salt. Cut in the margarine or pinch with your fingers until dough is crumbly. On a well-floured surface, roll the dough into an approximately ¼ inch / 6 mm high rectangle. Cut the pieces using the template and then sprinkle the cookies with granulated sugar. Place cookies on a baking sheet covered with parchment paper.
Bake at 400°F / 200°C until tops are covered with golden brown flecks.

Paper template

Thin cardboard, as from a cereal box
7½ in / 19 cm long
4 in / 10 cm wide at center over the "stomach"
Cut out a little triangle to use for holding the template as you cut out the cookies.

Keep kitchen fabrics such as old curtains, cloths, and decorative hand towels.

Reproduce them on paper with a photocopier and write out delightful pages with pretty embroidery that you can sew into the ideabook.

A recipe for pudding copied from Great-Grandmother's old cookbook. With gothic script and ragged edges, the recipe becomes a pretty entry in an ideabook. The page is copied from an old kitchen towel, and who knows, maybe the pudding is good also.

Make collages of inspiring pictures and glue in paper slips where you can write your own notes.

RENOVATE
AND RENEW

Do you have plans for building a new house or renovating an old one? Buying a new condo or fixing up the old one? It costs so little to dream and make plans. Cut out and glue in the pictures you find that give you something to dream about. Add pictures of before and after to document the entire process. We bought an old abandoned train station in 1999 and we documented all the renovations. We like to look through our pictures and show them to our guests.

Make sketches and take photos of the process whether your house is new or old. Not everyone would agree that renovating is fun, but the changes from "worn out" to "brand new" result in a good feeling. Take pictures of your dream house and interiors you like, and everything you want that you might own some day. Doesn't everyone need to dream now and then?

Here are some pictures of what we had and inspiration for what it could be. You're allowed to dream occasionally, and it costs so little to think big.

Make collages of things you like and colors you think you might use. Add fabric swatches and color samples. Looking back at the book and studying these pages is almost like going on a treasure hunt at a second-hand shop, but you can do it on your own sofa—and it's so much cheaper that way.

Book below: Cool photos found in the rafters up in the attic when we put in new insulation.

GENEALOGY IDEABOOK

Make an ideabook to hold the history of your parents, grandparents, great-grand-parents, uncles, and aunts. Trace and dig!

Magnhild Olsen Nijordet
født 24 april 1910.
Asmund Kristiansen Skahud
født 22 August 1899.
Søn
Ole Reidar Asmundsen Skahud
født 9. Januar 1930.

Nye Testa
og
Salmernes B

Skahud.

, 1915

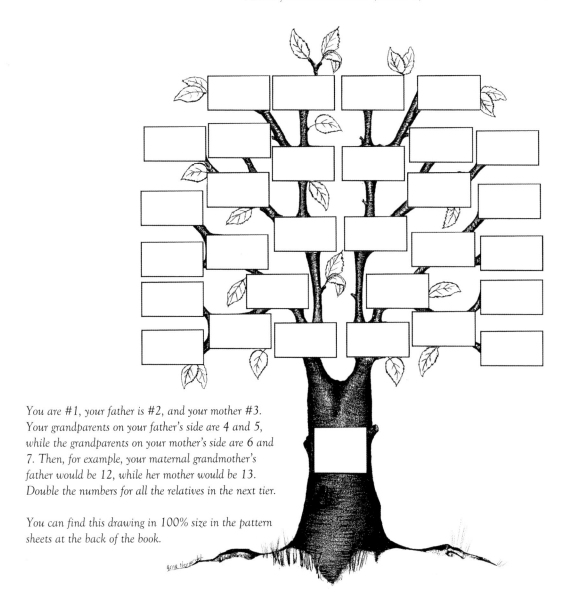

You are #1, your father is #2, and your mother #3.
Your grandparents on your father's side are 4 and 5,
while the grandparents on your mother's side are 6 and
7. Then, for example, your maternal grandmother's
father would be 12, while her mother would be 13.
Double the numbers for all the relatives in the next tier.

You can find this drawing in 100% size in the pattern
sheets at the back of the book.

Save old photos, baptismal certificates, and so on, and make copies to glue into the book. Don't forget to write down where you found the information and your sources, so that later on you can help someone who is double checking. Don't always believe everything you find on online genealogy pages. One mistake on the web can spread very quickly. Anyone can add information, so everything should always be double checked. Check parish records, folk histories, and old city records. Old family photos and prayer books can reveal new information.

Some useful sources on the web are www.ancestry.com (or ancestry.co.uk), www.geni.com, and www.myheritage.com.

Write down names and information about your ancestors, their children, grandchildren, and so on. That way, you might find some new relatives and people that you didn't know you were related to. Find out where they live, what they do, when they were born, and when they died. You might find the history of your relatives in old books, so write that down. Put in a little about the time they lived in, and save any photos of people, farms, and houses from that period. Old postcards of places where they lived are pretty in such books. Write and glue in everything about your family history to give life to your ancestors.

Carlos has ideabooks about his grandfather and great-grandfather. Little sketches of their houses and furniture, little watercolors, and pastel drawings were copied and glued in together with photos and dates.

Arne has a multiple great-great-great-great-great-grandfather mentioned in an adventure story, so the adventure got a place in his family ideabook. Anything that gives the family history some new life goes into the ideabook. The further back in time one goes, the more fun it is!

Family history is a fascinating hobby because you learn so much about yourself, and it's exciting to see how people used to live, what they did, and where they lived. It is also interesting to see what professions and choices are part of your heritage.

DRAW YOUR OWN STENCILS

The genealogy tree has four branches—the child's parents and four grandparents. Fill in what you know about the seven people on the tree. The great-grandparents can be the first on a new tree.

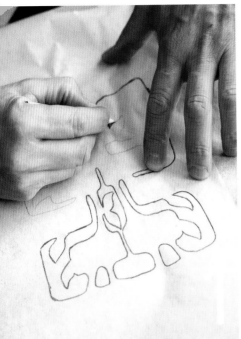
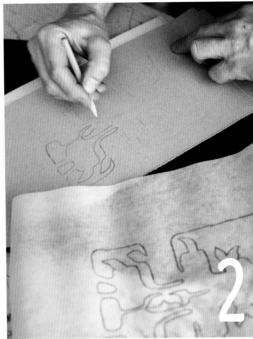

1   Use tracing or waxed paper and draw the tree onto a thin piece of cardboard.
    Empty cereal boxes are good for this.

2   Draw over the outline made from the tracing paper onto the cardboard if the
    impression is weak. *This drawing at 100% size is included on the pattern sheets in
    the back of this book.*

3   Cut out the tree.

4   Use a cutting board if you are afraid of damaging your table.

5   Cover the pages you don't want to spray, and attach the stencil you have cut out to the page with mounting
    spray. Spray the page and then go over it with a hair dryer before you remove the backing.

6   Remove the paper carefully and you have a tree ready to fill in.

7   Place two trees next to each other, so you can write your own name under the tree and then begin with your fa-
    ther's tree on the left side and your mother's on the right side. Your father's tree might have a blue background
    and your mother's tree red, if you want to be very traditional. A black background is stylish, too—or maybe
    try a brown tone so that the page looks a little old. Make two pages in your ideabook the same way, so you'll
    have space for yourself, your parents, four grandparents, and eight great-grandparents. After that all the great-
    grandparents can come up again on two new pages, with their parents, grandparents and great-grandparents.

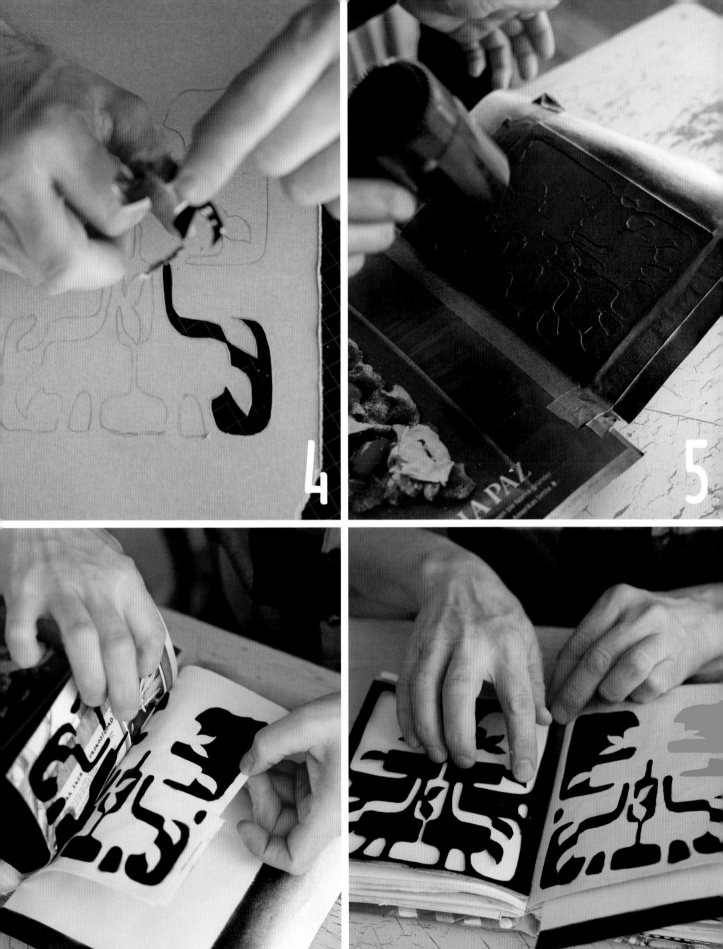

DECORATING THE PICTURES

Transforming one page with an old bank note. Here we used a homemade stencil to embellish the page. Both sides are painted with gold and blown dry. The lace is positioned on the page and then sprayed with white.

Some little variations of the tree design. The two below have blue and red circles to write numbers in—the blue circles are for your father's side and the red for your mother's.

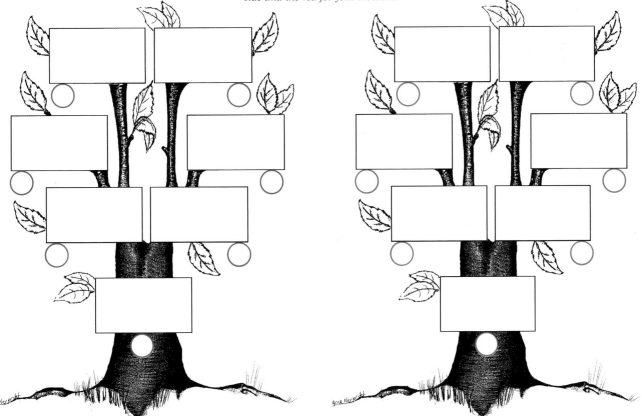

DECOUPAGE TECHNIQUE

Make a copy of an old photo and glue it to a piece of thin cardboard with decoupage glue (we used Royal Coat's finish from Panduro Hobby) if you want the picture to look the same as the original. Some colors disappear on regular copy paper. Blow-dry the picture and cut it out.

Glue the picture into the book and place a nice sheet of paper on the opposite page with space for information about the people in the picture.

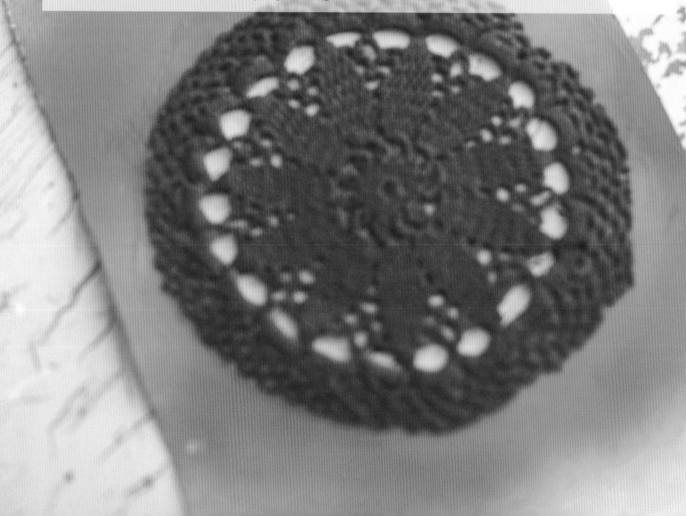

TRANSFERRING LACE MOTIFS

If you want, for example, to write the names of the children and grandchildren, designate all the children with letters.

For example, #12 and #13 have the children A: Kari, B: Ole, C: Knut, D: Mari. A: Kari's children would be A1, A2, A3, etc.

Kari's grandchildren would be A1A, A1B, A1C, etc.

You can repeat the sequence of letters and numbers as needed. Mark the page with the parents' number—for example, 12 and 13, who are the great-grandparents of the children on the mother's side. Mark the page with these numbers, find their letters on the tree and then you'll know who they are. The further back in time you go, the higher the numbers, and the more confusing it can be if you don't keep track of who your ancestors are.

Decorate the pages with stamps, photos, or other things that remind you of the person you are writing about. Copy old book pages and use them as a background for the photos—do not glue in originals. You can also use a product called Distress Ink (available from hobby shops) to make the pages look old. Blank stamps with frames are fine for printing onto the pages so you can write in numbers or names, or you can make your own frames with old lace. Here we've cut out a circle in the paper and glued in motifs from old crocheted doilies.

STAMP IDEABOOK

Stamps are pretty when glued in closely spaced together over entire pages, perhaps used only to decorate or possibly for inspiration. These collages can reveal pretty color combinations that you can then use in your handcraft projects.

Here are some pages we've decorated with postage stamps, both for inspiration and for color combinations. We especially like these miniature artworks because their visual effect becomes so fine when one arranges many stamps on one page.

Put the stamps in water to loosen them from the background paper. Let them dry completely before you glue them into an ideabook.

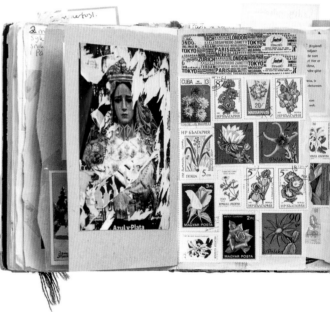

Here are some more of our favorite postage stamp pages.

GARDENING IDEABOOK

Collect sources of inspiration and gather your notes. Have an ideabook for writing down what you sowed or planted. Glue or pin in tags from the plants you bought or the empty seed packets. You can also make your own seed packets and collect seeds in the fall.

We almost never know what we've planted when our perennial seeds sprout one fine day. For that reason, it's expedient to have something written down somewhere. Sometimes you might also need pictures to find out what the plant is called, especially if it came in a packet without a picture.

A gardening ideabook is great to write in, not only so you can find out what you have in the garden but also as inspiration for new gardening projects.

GERANIUM

Ballerina

Album

Wlassovianum

Renard

Johnson Blue

Max Frei

Baby Blue

Samobor

Chambridge

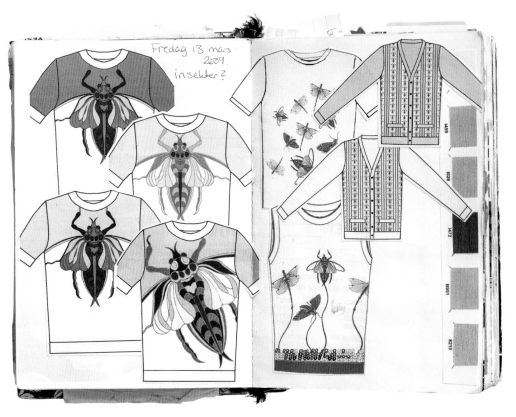

Old designs we made inspired by the garden.

A pretty background from the garden found in a leaf, a new geranium for the collection, and a pressed flower from the garden; masking tape imprinted with flowers holds loose edges in place or covers old notes.

Flowers and leaves from your own garden can also be used as stencils in an ideabook. Embellish a tabloid-size page (11 x 17) and divide the pages at the center to letter size (8.5 x 11/A4). The fold will give you four new pages for the ideabook. Mix them with other sheets so that they make new pictures.

Garden inspiration.

A knitted pillow cover inspired from the garden pages in our ideabooks.

CROCHET
IDEABOOK

When we decide to go through our yarn after a long winter, we often end up using the leftovers to crochet a new throw. Butterflies are a theme we work with a lot and these granny squares have a butterfly shaping.

Granny squares for inspiration. The garments were made from leftover yarns by Xuly Bet, the designer who made recycling fashionable in the 1990s.

We often mix handcrafts and garden work. Here's a crocheted flower inspired by our garden.

Make your own sewing ideabook. We like quilting squares in various techniques and we gather our thoughts with pretty pictures for inspiration. Quilting is one of our hobbies. Take a look at our ideabook and perhaps you'll also be inspired.

SEWING IDEABOOK

An old pattern sheet decorating a sewing ideabook. A template for a hexagonal quilt block is at the ready, clipped in for the next time we want to work on this project. You can find a template for the hexagon in the pattern sheets at the back of this book.

We like imaginative techniques the best. These pieces were sewn from fabrics that had been used as insulation around the windows in Arne's childhood home. Pretty fabric remnants and cloth were wrapped around all the windows. Arne saved the fabrics when the windows were replaced many years ago. We washed them, ironed them, and sewed quilt squares with them in all sorts of fantastic techniques. They were then added to our old ideabooks. They were a little too pretty to be used as rags or thrown away, or for anything other than embellishment of an ideabook.

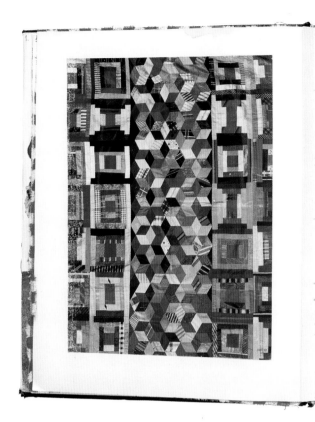

In one of our first ideabooks, we saved some patchwork pictures from old fashion magazines.

Pretty pictures and patterns for inspiration. Some old text is painted over with acrylic paint and an old note on the acrylic paint is covered over with masking tape. Layer upon layer.

TRAVEL IDEABOOK

Collect the items you can't glue in while traveling.

A Polaroid camera is nice to have on a trip and the day's photos can be glued in that evening. If you don't have a camera like this, leave space for pictures on the pages so they can be glued in later. Glue an envelope into the ideabook to store any items you can't glue in on the trip. Also save space for the pictures. Save ads, especially those with decorative writing. If the page you want to use is smaller than the ad, tear advertising paper off in the right size and glue the paper in as a background. Glue in tickets and anything else you want to save or decorate an ideabook with, or put everything into an envelope until later. Our travel ideabooks are never pure travelogues—we'd never be able to be so orderly with our things! At the same time, our books are part of our work, so we might also add in knitting ideas or some notes about something we knitted in between our travel notes.

A trip to Japan resulted in many pretty items for an ideabook. Wrapping paper, advertisements, and old paper all became part of this one.

Make drawings of your travel impressions. Always take a black India ink pen on any trip.

This ideabook has been in Paris.

Chocolate wrapper from the duty-free shop in a European airport, and pictures from
vinyl records that we want in our collection (they are crossed out when we find the records).

Pretty graffiti walls photographed in New York City.

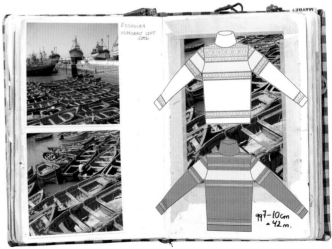

In Peru we climbed a mountain 16,109 feet / 4910 meters above sea level, ate alpaca, and visited a monastery. Everything was documented in our own way.

Knitting inspired by the colors from a trip to Morocco.

HORSE IDEABOOK

Horses are one of our favorite themes. We collect horse images, and have used our horses in many designs. Here is Arne's father with Blakka. His sweater has a pattern from the 1950s but it was knitted in the purple phase of the 1980s. The sketches of the striped sweaters with horses are from a summer collection we produced in 2009.

Horse embroidery inspired by a rocking horse in a photo from an interior design magazine.

We found this rocking horse in a second-hand store a few years ago. The seller told us that he had once had two of them, one with a blue saddle and underside and the other in red. He had bought them from a man who had given his son the blue one and his daughter the red one as gifts sometime in the 1950s. We have used the horse on a t-shirt print and for pillow embroidery.

HOBBY IDEABOOK

Make your own hobby ideabook and collect your interests.

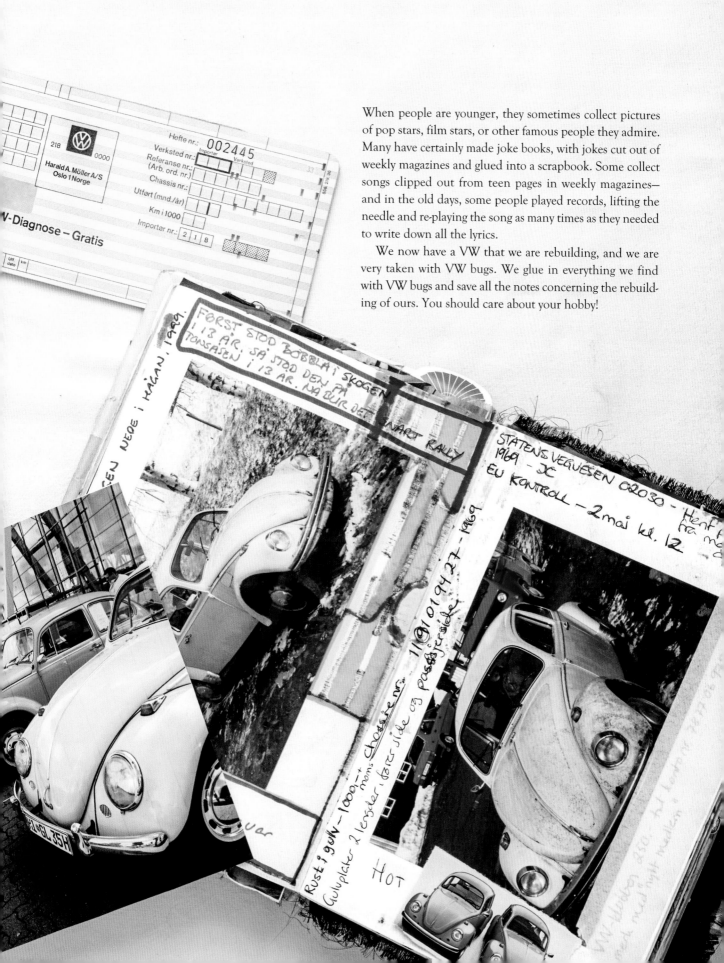

When people are younger, they sometimes collect pictures of pop stars, film stars, or other famous people they admire. Many have certainly made joke books, with jokes cut out of weekly magazines and glued into a scrapbook. Some collect songs clipped out from teen pages in weekly magazines—and in the old days, some people played records, lifting the needle and re-playing the song as many times as they needed to write down all the lyrics.

We now have a VW that we are rebuilding, and we are very taken with VW bugs. We glue in everything we find with VW bugs and save all the notes concerning the rebuilding of ours. You should care about your hobby!

BRIDAL IDEABOOK

Weddings require a lot of planning. At the absolute least, the dress is very important. We have designed some bridal dresses and it's no laughing matter. A few examples are needed to choose from. Save any inspiration, such as fabric swatches or ribbons. Save the inspiration for table coverings and bouquets and document the entire process. Make your own bridal ideabook. Glue in photos from the planning, the wedding, and the honeymoon.

Inspiration for a bridal dress.

Sketches of bridal gowns with swatches of fabric and ribbon.

ACTIVITY IDEABOOK

This is perhaps the last thing you do before your magazines go into the recycling bin. Cut out all the things and activities you find and sort them alphabetically. Make it simple for small children. Juxtapose magazine pictures with glossy photos, labels, and and anything else you can cut out.

We are not in total agreement about how fun this is—one of us sometimes feels that it can be irritating when the other asks him to find things that start with B. If you are happy to cut and glue, it's a good excuse for exactly that: to cut and glue, which can be a pleasant and enjoyable activity.

FINALLY

We hope you will be as happy to make your own ideabooks as we have been. Perhaps you have been inspired to find other useful themes for your ideabooks. We hope these homemade books can be a release for you at a time when everything is shared on the internet.

Thanks to photographer Ragnar Hartvig and stylist Ingrid Ullstad Skaansar, who are now in one of our books along with us.

SHOPPING LIST

You can find most of the materials you'll need as well as our starter packs for your book at Panduro Hobby. www.pandurohobby.com

We use the following products for our books:

Allround Glue, article 220593

Allround Glue stick, article 220553

Quickglue, article 220509

Wood glue, article 220557

Decoupage glue, Royal Coat Finish, article 220594

Spray glue, quick-drying, article 210155

Edding Spray Lacquer – available in at least 30 colors,

all article numbers begin with 1820xx

At Panduro Hobby and other craft shops, you will also find self-adhesive textile sheets to use on book covers. This might be a good alternative for anyone who doesn't want to work with glue. We also recommend second-hand shops where you can always find old lace fabrics, curtains, and crocheted doilies that work well.

Mounting spray can be purchased at art or office supply stores.

Wing screws and boards for making your own book press can be found at stores selling art materials or at hardware stores.

We are interactive! Visit our new site at www.arne-carlos.com to become better acquainted with us and find even more inspiration.

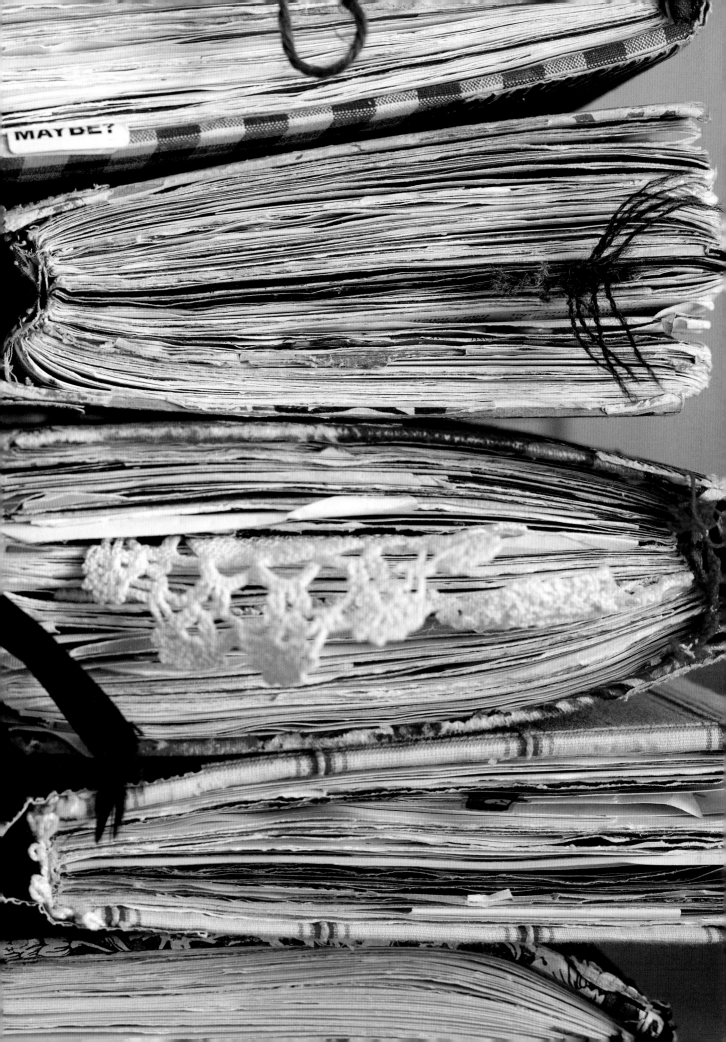

MAYBE?